THE FRANK W. PIERCE MEMORIAL LECTURES

AT CORNELL UNIVERSITY, OCTOBER 1966

Strategic Factors in Economic Development

The Frank W. Pierce Memorial Lectureship, at the New York State School of Industrial and Labor Relations at Cornell University, is made possible through the generosity of the Teagle Foundation, Incorporated.

PUBLISHED BY

New York State School of Industrial and Labor Relations
A Statutory College of the State University of New York
at Cornell University

Italy: School for Awakening Countries
by Maurice F. Neufeld   600 pp. $9.00 cloth

Poor Countries and Authoritarian Rule
by Maurice F. Neufeld   256 pp. $5.00 cloth

Élites, Intellectuals, and Consensus: Chile
by James O. Morris   312 pp. $6.00 cloth

Industrial Wages in Chile
by Peter Gregory   128 pp. $5.50 cloth
                                           $3.00 paper

An Introduction to Japanese Trade Unionism
by Alice H. Cook   228 pp. $5.00 paper

Bibliography of Industrial Relations in Latin America
by James O. Morris and Efrén Córdova   308 pp. $10.00 cloth

Strategic Factors in Economic Development
By Nicholas Kaldor   96 pp. $2.50 cloth

Order from Distribution Center

Strategic Factors in

Economic Development

NICHOLAS KALDOR

*Professor of Economics at
the University of Cambridge*

AND

Fellow of King's College

New York State School of Industrial and Labor
Relations, Cornell University, Ithaca, New York

1967

Copyright © 1967 by Cornell University

Library of Congress Catalog Card Number: 67-65424

Price: $2.50

ORDER FROM

Distribution Center, New York State School
of Industrial and Labor Relations,
Cornell University, Ithaca, New York

PRINTED IN THE UNITED STATES OF AMERICA
W. F. HUMPHREY PRESS, INC., GENEVA, NEW YORK

Preface

I

THE field of industrial and labor relations is often viewed narrowly as management-employee relations, involving mainly the day-by-day accommodation of management and labor's interests in the workplace, but sometimes punctuated by dramatic conflict. To the layman, the issues appear to grow out of ideological differences, failures of leadership, and inadequate communication, and in fact these explanations are partially true.

Yet, the industrial and labor relations drama must be examined within a larger setting. Managers and union leaders are merely actors, protagonists and antagonists, reflecting the personal and institutional needs and interests of people caught up in sweeping events which quite transcend the demands and counterdemands of the moment. Labor conflict, no matter how dramatic, is but a brief encounter, highlighting areas of tension within a framework of relationships of considerably greater scope.

There are few persons with the breadth of practical experience and the analytic capacity to abstract structure and meaning from the myriad human relationships that constitute a national and world economy. Professor Nicholas Kaldor is such a person, combining both academic and practical interests. He is professor of economics at the University of Cambridge and a fellow of King's College. He has written extensively on such topics as economic stability and growth, tax reform, capital accumulation, and full employment.

Professor Kaldor has served his country and the world community with distinction. He has been an economic and fiscal advisor to many nations including India, Mexico, Ceylon, and Turkey. From 1947 to 1949, he was director of the Research and Planning Division of the Economic Commission for Europe and from 1951 to 1955 served on England's Royal Commission on Taxation of Profits and Income. He was a member of the Economic Commission for Latin America in 1956, and in 1963 he was a visiting economist at the Reserve Bank of Australia. For the past several years, Professor Kaldor has been a special advisor on taxation to the Chancellor of the Exchequer in England.

No stranger to the United States, Professor Kaldor had a Rockefeller Traveling Fellowship in the United States in 1935–1936 and was a Ford visiting research professor at the University of California, Berkeley, in 1959–1960.

Professor Kaldor's three lectures on strategic

factors in economic development are directed primarily to the professional economist, but his ideas can be readily grasped by the layman. His basic proposition is that differences in economic growth among countries cannot be explained simply on the basis of the "efficiency of business management, the nature and quality of education, the vitality or creativity of the population, the framework of political institutions." He looks rather to certain economic constraints that limit growth at various stages of development. He sees growth as peculiarly associated with the industrial activities of the economy and asks the important question, what stimulates or limits the development of these activities in an economy? In his lectures, he seeks answers to this question not only with regard to advanced countries but also with regard to the underdeveloped areas of the world.

One might ask whether Professor Kaldor's sweeping analysis has anything to do with industrial and labor relations. It does indeed. It sheds light on the labor structure of economies in various stages of development and, more important, on the dynamics of change in this structure. It sets forth the very interesting proposition that industrial growth is constrained and limited as the income per capita in the service or tertiary sector of the economy approaches that in the manufacturing sector. It underscores in this and other ways the importance of labor supply to the manufacturing sector and the relationship of the movement and availability of labor to wage and salary policy. It points up the parallel between the importation of goods from low-wage economies and the introduction of labor-saving technologies and inventions. As Professor Kaldor puts it, "the effects of imports from the low-wage countries on the real income of recipient countries is in no way different from the effect of labor-saving inventions of any kind."

All of these propositions have important implications for management-employee relations.

II

Professor Kaldor's lectures at Cornell University are a noteworthy beginning to a lecture series in industrial and labor relations called the Frank W. Pierce Memorial Lectureship. The Pierce Lectureship was established at the New York State School of Industrial and Labor Relations at Cornell through a generous grant from the Teagle Foundation. Because of Mr. Pierce's outstanding and pioneering career in personnel management, it seemed altogether fitting that the lectureship should be sponsored by Cornell's School of Industrial and Labor Relations on whose council Mr. Pierce served with distinction for many years.

The faculty of the School was doubly pleased with the opportunity, on the one hand, to initiate and guide a new lecture series at Cornell dealing with important aspects of the urban, industrial society in which we live and, on the other hand, to honor a great Cornellian who distinguished himself in the industrial and labor relations field over a period of more than forty years.

Mr. Frank Willis Pierce was born in Olean, New York, in 1893. He received the degree of Mechanical Engineer from Cornell in 1916. Like many other good Cornellians, he adapted his basic university education to new and developing fields. Rather early in his career, he moved into administrative activities, organizing Goodyear Tire and Rubber Company's War Service Department during World War I. In 1924, he joined Standard Oil Company (New Jersey) as industrial relations advisor.

At Standard Oil, Pierce was named assistant to the president and head of industrial relations in 1933 and also served as a director of the company from 1942 until his retirement in 1954.

He served as a director and chairman of the board of Imperial Oil Limited, of Toronto, Canadian affiliate of Standard Oil Company (New Jersey) from 1944 to 1948.

Mr. Pierce was affiliated with Industrial Relations Counselors, Inc., a non-profit research and education firm in New York City founded in 1946.

Among his other activities were membership on the Advisory Council of the New York State School of Industrial and Labor Relations at Cornell and on the Cornell University Council from 1951 to 1962; he also gave time and effort to the Department of Church and Economic Life of the National Council of Churches.

Those who know the history of modern personnel management know that Mr. Pierce's career spanned the entire period of its development from World War I to the present decade.

The lectureship is underwritten by a $100,000 grant from the Teagle Foundation, established by the late Walter C. Teagle, himself a Cornellian. The School's faculty is keenly aware of the trust and responsibility accorded it by the Teagle Foundation in honoring Mr. Pierce who was a trustee of the Foundation from its inception.

DAVID G. MOORE, *Dean*
New York State School of
Industrial and Labor Relations

Contents

LECTURE I

The Role of Increasing

Returns in Industry

THESE LECTURES will discuss why the economies
of some countries grow so much faster than others.
The very fact that the world at present is so sharply
divided between "rich" and "poor" countries is, in
the context of the broad sweep of history, something
relatively new: it is the cumulative result of the
historical experience of two or three hundred years.
If we go back a few hundred years for example, to
1700 or 1750, we do not find, as far as we can tell,
such large differences in real income per capita between different countries or regions. The populations of most countries lived at about a subsistence
level—they all had the appearance of underdeveloped countries, by present-day standards. Differences
in natural endowment in climate or the fertility of
the soil were fairly well balanced by differences in
the density of population; and the great majority of

the population of *all* countries derived their living from primary production, that is, from agriculture. But starting in the middle of the 18th century, a particular group of countries of Western Europe experienced annual or decennial rates of economic growth, which, according to Professor Kuznets, were thirty to forty times as large as those experienced over the previous seventeen centuries since the birth of Christ. Though their populations also grew at ten to twenty times the previous rate, the growth of production far outstripped the growth of population and the standard of living rose substantially—it trebled or more in each century. This process of rapid growth gradually extended to the settlements of Europeans in America, and later to Oceania; in the late 19th century it encompassed Russia and Japan. In the present century the growth rates of the fast-growing countries have tended to accelerate even further.

In the rest of the world, the rhythm of development has been far from even. The rate of economic growth in many countries has barely kept pace with the growth of populations; indeed, in some countries, such as India or Pakistan, it has failed to keep pace, so that the general standard of living, as far as one can ascertain, has been falling rather than rising in the last century. The current vast differences in living standards—recently estimated at nearly 30:1 or even 50:1 between the countries at the top of the

4

scale and those at the bottom of the scale—are large-ly the result of the fast growth rates over the past two to three hundred years of a certain group of countries and the virtual stagnation of the other countries. There is also an intermediary range of semidevel-oped countries, many in Latin America, which have experienced fast growth rates for a period, but which have failed to maintain the pace of development for very long.

Moreover we observe large differences in growth rates among the developed or industrialized coun-tries themselves. If we take the decade 1953/4–1963/4, (that is, starting from a year when most countries had regained or exceeded their pre-World War II level of production) we find very considerable differences in the rates of growth. At one end of the scale, two highly developed countries, the United States and the United Kingdom, grew at a rate of 3 percent a year or less. At the other end of the scale, Japan grew at a rate of 10 percent a year, and there was a group of countries (West Germany, Italy, France, and Austria) the rate of growth of which was around 5 to 6 percent a year. A larger number of smaller countries, such as Denmark, Norway, Netherlands, and Belgium, grew at annual rates of between 3 and 4½ percent. If we take the last five years, the picture is somewhat different. Japan remains outstanding with a growth rate of around 10 percent, a large number of countries (including the United States) grew at between 4½ and 5½ percent a year, while the United Kingdom has shown a rate of growth of only 3.3 percent.

Economic theory, and particularly the theory of economic growth on which so much important work has been done in recent years, has little to offer to explain such differences. It can point to a large number of economic, sociological, and political factors which are relevant to the problem, such as the efficiency of business management, the nature and quality of education, the general social milieu, the vitality or creativity of the population, the framework of political institutions, and so on, but there is no general agreement as to which of these factors plays the major role. In our present state of knowledge there is no way in which such hypotheses could be tested and their role in any way be quantified. My own feeling is that at different stages of economic development, different kinds of constraints (or limitations) operate, and, although some of these factors are sociological or political in origin, the major explanation is likely to be an economic one. Basically, it may be described in terms of the varying nature of the responses of supply to changes in demand, and of the responses of demand that result from changes in supply.

Contrary to the usual procedure—and for reasons which may become evident later—I shall analyze the problem first in the context of the so-called developed countries, the relatively small group of countries with a high real income per capita. I shall then apply this method to analyze the obstacles to the development of the underdeveloped countries, and, finally, in the context of the growth of the world economy as a whole.

One of the best known generalizations in economics is that development involves a continued fall in the share of the "primary" sector in total output and employment and a continued rise in the share of the "secondary" and "tertiary" sectors. In the primary sector everybody includes agriculture; for reasons that will become evident later, I also include mining. By secondary sector I mean industry which is mainly manufacturing, but also included are construction and public utilities. The tertiary sector is the name given to services of the most varied kinds from domestic servants to university professors, from transport and distribution to banks, insurance, and so on.

Put briefly, the contention that I intend to examine is that fast rates of economic growth are almost invariably associated with the fast rate of growth of the secondary sector, mainly, manufacturing, and that this is an attribute of an intermediate stage of development; it is a characteristic of the transition from "immaturity" to "maturity." The term "maturity" is meant to denote, not just a high level of real income per capita, but a state of affairs where real income per capita, including profits as well as wages, has reached broadly the same level in the three sectors. (In this latter sense Britain has reached a higher degree of maturity than the United States.)

I shall begin by examining the empirical evidence in favor of my contention; I shall then discuss the theoretical reasons to justify it; and finally its implication in terms of the potential growth rates of the advanced countries.

Let us then begin with the evidence. If we take twelve industrially advanced countries in the ten years 1953–1954 to 1963–1964, shown in Table 1,[1] we find that there is a very high correlation between the rate of growth of the gross domestic product and the rate of growth of manufacturing production. Even more significant, we find that the faster the overall rate of growth, the greater is the *excess* of the rate of growth of manufacturing production over the rate of growth of the economy as a whole. Expressing this in terms of a regression equation with the rate of growth of G.D.P. (Y) as a function of the rate of growth of manufacturing output (X) we get the relationship

$$Y = 1.153 + 0.614X, \quad R^2 = 0.959$$
$$(0.040)$$

[1]The twelve countries were chosen because they were all members of the Organization for Economic Cooperation and Development (O.E.C.D.) and comparable figures were available. A comprehensive list of "developed" countries (outside the Communist

Increasing Returns in Industry

Table 1. Rate of Growth of G.D.P. and Rate of Growth of Manufacturing Production.

Twelve Industrial Countries, Average 1953–1954 to Average 1963–1964

	*Annual Rate of Growth of G.D.P.**	Exponential growth rates *Annual Rate of Growth of Manufacturing Production**
Japan	9.6	13.6†
Italy	5.6	8.2
West Germany	6.0	7.3
Austria	5.4	6.2
France	4.9	5.6
Netherlands	4.5	5.5‡
Belgium	3.6	5.1
Denmark	4.1	4.9
Norway	3.9	4.6
Canada	3.6	3.4
U.K.	2.7	3.2
U.S.A.	3.1	2.6

Sources: National Accounts Statistics, O.E.C.D.; National Accounts Yearbooks, U.N.

*Derived from National Accounts Data of G.D.P., and G.D.P. in Manufacturing, at constant prices.

†Index of Manufacturing Production.

‡G.D.P. in Industrial Production (including mining).

Regression: Growth of G.D.P. (Y) on Growth of Manufacturing Output (X)

$$Y = 1.153 + 0.614 \ X \qquad R^2 = .959$$
$$(0.040)$$

Standard Error of residuals as a proportion of mean value of $Y = .0825$

world) should have included two more O.E.C.D. members (Sweden and Switzerland) as well as at least three others (Australia, New Zealand, and Finland).

Factors in Economic Development

The high value of the correlation coefficient and the fact that the standard error is less than one-tenth of the regression coefficient indicates that this is a statistically significant relationship, on the basis of which one should be able to predict fairly accurately the rate of growth of an economy if one knows the rate of growth of its manufacturing production.[2]

That the growth of manufacturing output and the growth of the G.D.P. should be highly correlated is not perhaps surprising, since manufacturing forms a large part (25 to 40 percent) of the total G.D.P. of the countries considered. But more surprising is the fact that the regression coefficient is significantly *less* than unity. Together with the positive constant in the equation, this implies that rates of growth of G.D.P. of more than 3 percent a year are found only in those cases where the rate of growth in manufacturing output is *in excess* of the rate of growth of the non-manufacturing sectors. That is, we find the rate of economic growth to be correlated with the

---

[2]The equation predicts the rate of growth of G.D.P. in the U.S. and the U.K. accurately for 1960–65; also for Germany and Canada within a small margin. For the two years 1963–1965 the relationship between the calculated and the observed figure is less close, particularly for the U.K.

G.D.P.

	1960–65		1963–65	
	Calculated	*Observed*	*Calculated*	*Observed*
U.S.	4.52	4.5	5.43	5.2
U.K.	2.97	3.14	4.49	3.8
Germany	4.57	4.77	4.77	4.77
Canada	5.44	5.25	6.35	6.1

excess of the rate of growth of manufacturing output over the rate of growth of the non-manufacturing sectors. This again could be shown in terms of a regression equation which is statistically significant. The experience of twelve countries over a ten-year period is not perhaps adequate to establish the universality of such a "law." I have not been able to extend it to a larger number of countries nor to investigate to what degree this has been true of earlier historical periods. Miss Deborah Paige, in a paper published in 1961, however, found evidence of the same kind of relationship over longer periods from the end of the 19th century onward.[3]

One should not of course attribute causal significance to a statistical relationship unless it can be shown to be consistent with some general hypothesis, supported by other evidence. Changes in the working population were not large enough to explain the differences in overall growth rates; these were largely accounted for by differences in the rates of growth of output-per-man, or "productivity." Is there some general hypothesis which would explain why the rate of increase of output-per-man, for an economy as a whole, should vary with the rate of growth of manufacturing production? One possible explanation is that the *level* of productivity in manufacturing activities is higher than in the rest of the economy. As a result, a faster expansion of the high-productivity

[3]Deborah Paige, "Economic Growth: The Last Hundred Years," London, *National Institute Economic Review*, July 1961, p. 41.

manufacturing sectors involving a faster rate of transfer of labor from the others will pull up the average. Similarly, one could argue that the incidence of technical progress, as measured by the rates of growth of productivity, is higher in manufacturing activities than in other fields, so that a greater concentration of labor in manufacturing tends to bring about a higher average rate of productivity growth.

These factors are not capable in themselves, however, of explaining the observed differences. Beckerman has shown in a recent book[4] that the changes in the distribution of labor between high and low productivity sectors can only account for a small part of the observed differences in productivity growth rates. Nor is it necessarily true that the rate of growth of productivity is higher in the manufacturing sector than in the other sectors. Productivity in manufacturing generally rises faster than in services; but in many of the countries, the rate of growth of productivity in agriculture and mining has been higher than in manufacturing or even in industrial activities taken as a whole.

There is another possible explanation—that productivity increases *in response to* increases in total output because of economies of scale or increasing returns. The idea that manufacturing activities were subject to the "law of increasing returns" was a major

---

[4]Wilfred Beckerman, *The British Economy in 1975* (Cambridge: Cambridge University Press, 1965), pp. 23–25.

contention of the classical economists. This proposition occupies the pride of place in the first three chapters of the *Wealth of Nations*. Adam Smith argued in that book that the *return* per unit of labor (what we now call productivity) depended on the division of labor—on specialization, which he elaborated in his famous example of pinmaking. He also emphasized that the division of labor depended on the extent of the market. The greater the market, the greater the differentiation and specialization, and the higher the "return." Neoclassical writers, with one or two famous exceptions such as Alfred Marshall and Allyn Young (two of the best known economists of Cambridge and Cornell) tended to ignore or to underemphasize this relationship. As Hahn and Matthews remarked in a recent article reviewing modern growth theories, "the reason for the neglect is no doubt the difficulty of fitting increasing returns into the prevailing framework of perfect competition and marginal productivity factor pricing."[5]

Adam Smith, Alfred Marshall, and Allyn Young have all stressed the interplay of static and dynamic factors in causing returns to increase in response to an increase in the scale of industrial activities. Greater division of labor is more productive, partly because it carries with it the development of more skill

---

[5]F. H. Hahn and R. C. O. Matthews, "The Theory of Economic Growth: A Survey," *Economic Journal,* Vol. LXXIV, December 1964, p. 833.

and know-how, which, in turn, lead to more innovations and improvements in design. We cannot really separate the effects of economies of large scale which are due to indivisibilities of various kinds (in principle, reversible) from those effects which are due to irreversible improvements in technology associated with a process of expansion. Learning is itself the product of experience. The faster the growth of investment and output, the faster the rate of growth of productivity owing to the process of "learning by doing."[6]

In addition, as Allyn Young emphasized in one of the outstanding classics on this difficult subject, increasing returns is a "macro-phenomenon." Precisely because so much of the economies of scale result from increased differentiation, new processes, and new subsidiary industries, they cannot be "discerned adequately by observing the effects of variations in the size of an individual firm or of a particular industry." Economies of scale are derived not only from the expansion of any single industry but from a general industrial expansion, which should be seen, as Young put it, "as an interrelated whole." With the extension of the division of labor, "the representative firm, like the industry of which it is a part, loses its identity."[7]

[6]Kenneth Arrow, "The Economic Implications of Learning by Doing," *Review of Economic Studies,* June 1962, pp. 155–173.

[7]Allyn Young, "Increasing Returns and Economic Progress," *Economic Journal,* December 1928, p. 538–9.

Increasing Returns in Industry

I believe this to be the fundamental explanation of the empirical relationship between productivity growth and output growth, a relationship which, named after the author of an early paper on it, is sometimes described as the "Verdoorn Law."[8] Largely because technological progress enters into it, not just the economies of large-scale production, it is a dynamic relationship concerned with the *rates of change* of productivity and output, rather than being a static relationship relating the *level* of productivity to the *scale* of output. Since Verdoorn's work, these phenomena have been investigated by others, including Salter in his work on *Productivity and Technical Change*[9] and, more recently, Beckerman.[10] But, as far as I can see, none of these authors has paid enough attention to the fact that the relationship is peculiarly associated with industrial activities (manufacturing, public utilities, construction) rather than with the primary or tertiary sectors of the economy.

Table 2 shows the growth rates of production, employment, and productivity in manufacturing industry for our twelve countries in the period from 1953–1954 to 1963–1964. The relationships are summarized in two regression equations, employment growth on output growth and productivity growth

[8]P. J. Verdoorn, "Fattori che regolano lo sviluppo della produttività del lavoro," *L'Industria*, 1949.

[9]W. E. G. Salter, *Productivity and Technical Change* (Cambridge: Cambridge University Press, 1960).

[10]Beckerman, pp. 221–228.

Factors in Economic Development

Table 2. Rates of Growth of Production, Employment, and Productivity in Manufacturing Industry.

Twelve Countries, Average 1953–1954 to Average 1963–1964

	Production*	Annual exponential growth rates Employment†	Productivity‡
Japan	13.6	5.8	7.8
Italy‖	8.1	3.9§	4.2
West Germany	7.4	2.8	4.5
Austria**	6.4	2.2	4.2
France‖	5.7	1.8	3.8
Denmark#	5.7	2.5§	3.2
Netherlands††	5.5	1.4	4.1
Belgium	5.1	1.2§	3.9
Norway	4.6	0.2	4.4
Canada	3.4	2.1	1.3
U.K.	3.2	0.4	2.8
U.S.A.**	2.6	0.0	2.6

Sources: National Account and Manpower Statistics, O.E.C.D. Monthly Bulletin of Statistics, U.N.

　*Gross Domestic Product, in manufacturing, at constant prices.

　†Wage and salary earners adjusted for changes in weekly manhours.

　‡Output per manhour, derived from first two columns.

　§Incorporates estimated change in weekly manhours.

　‖1954–5 — 1963–4

　#1955–6 — 1963–4

　**1953–4 — 1962–3

　††Industrial Production and Employment (including Mining).

Regressions:

　*Rate of growth of Productivity (P) on the rate of growth of manufacturing production (X)

$$P = 1.035 + 0.484 \text{ X} \qquad R^2 = .826$$
$$(0.070)$$

　†Rate of growth of Employment (E) on rate of growth of manufacturing production (X)

$$E = -1.028 + 0.516 \text{ X} \qquad R^2 = .844$$
$$(0.070)$$

on output growth. Each of these equations is sufficiently significant, judged by the correlation coefficients and the standard errors, to suggest the view
that the growth of output must have played a major
part in the determination of the productivity growth
rates. (These two regression equations are, of course,
merely two ways of looking at the same thing. But
for rounding errors the regression coefficients of the
two equations should add to unity, and the two constants to zero.) Though the experience of the different countries has been far from uniform—some
countries, such as Belgium or Norway, managed to
increase their production with a proportionately
much smaller contribution from increased manpower than the average, while others, such as Canada
or Italy, required a proportionately greater contribution—the regression equations do suggest that there
is statistically a highly significant relationship. The
equations suggest that each percentage addition to
the growth of output requires a .5 percent increase
in employment in manhours and is associated with a
.5 percent increase in productivity. These coefficients
agree closely with those of Verdoorn, and, indeed, of
other investigators.

There are some economists who, although admit-
ting the validity of the Verdoorn Law as a statistical
relationship, argue that it can say nothing about
cause and effect. According to their view, the causal
relationship might well be the other way round. That
is, it may simply reflect the fact that a faster growth

rate in productivity induces, *via* its effects on relative costs and prices, a faster rate of growth of demand.

This alternative hypothesis is not, however, fully specified. If the rate of growth of productivity in each industry and in each country were a fully autonomous factor, it would still need to be explained. The usual assumption is that the rate of advance of science and technology is the main factor determining the rate of productivity growth. But this assumption is hardly appropriate for explaining large differences in the *same* industry over the *same* period in *different* countries. For instance, over the period 1954–1960, productivity in the automobile industry increased at 7 percent a year in Germany and at only 2.7 percent in Britain. Since the same United States firms (Ford and General Motors) controlled large segments of the industry in both countries, it would be difficult to explain such differences in terms of different access to new knowledge or "know-how." Besides, the role of economies of scale is too well-known in the automobile industry for its influence to be denied, quite apart from the Verdoorn Law.

Furthermore, to defend the hypothesis that productivity growth is simply due to advance in science and technology, we would need to go much further than postulating that productivity growth rates were autonomous. We would also have to assume that different productivity growth rates between different industries and sectors are fully reflected in movements of relative prices (not in movements of relative wages and earnings). A further assumption would have to be that the price elasticity of demand was *always* greater than unity, whether for the output of any one industry or for the output of manufacturing industry as a whole. Otherwise, there would be no more reason to expect that the growth of output should *exceed* the growth of productivity than that it should fall short of it. I am quite sure that if this alternative hypothesis were fully specified, and submitted to econometric tests, it would be conclusively refuted.

Once we recognize the relationship between productivity growth and output growth, the large differences in recorded productivity growth rates seem less startling, and we get a different impression of the "efficiency ranking" of our twelve countries. Thus, in the period considered, the rate of growth of productivity in manufacturing industry of the United States at 2.6 percent per year was one of the lowest, even lower than the United Kingdom. Yet this figure was greater, about 13 percent greater, than that which can be computed from the Verdoorn regression equation for the twelve countries. This indicates that, given the fact of the United States' low rate of growth of industrial production as determined by demand, its performance was considerably better than the average. By the same test the performance of the United Kingdom was slightly better than average. Of the other countries, Norway was outstanding with a recorded rate of growth of productivity fully one-third greater than could be expected, while Canada's performance was outstandingly poor, with a rate of productivity growth only one-half as high as the computed figure. The record of the Netherlands and Belgium was moderately good, with the recorded rates 12 to 13 percent higher than the average, and Italy and Denmark were moderately poor performers, with a deficiency of around 15 percent.

All this is subject, of course, to the statistical difficulties inherent in all international comparisons, and many of the deviations are too small to be of much significance in judging the countries' performances. The interesting fact is that with the sole exception of Canada, the deviations appear to be significantly related to investment behavior. The outstanding performer, Norway, invested very heavily in relation to her growth rate, while the poor performers, Italy and Denmark, were also the relatively low investors. Thus, if we look for the effects of investment behavior on productivity growth, not in terms of the growth rate itself, but according to the deviation of an individual country's performance from the Verdoorn regression line, the effects of relatively high or low investment on productivity growth are far more readily discernible.[11]

---

[11]See note *(c)* in the Statistical Appendix at the end of this volume.

Increasing Returns in Industry

I would not like to imply that the Verdoorn Law applies exclusively to manufacturing activities, nor, indeed, that it applies to each manufacturing industry individually. Outside the industrial field, however, it is far less in evidence. It certainly does not apply to agriculture or mining, where the statistics show the growth of productivity to have been much in excess of the growth in output. Indeed, production growth and employment growth tend to be related negatively, rather than positively, in these two sectors. The classical economists always asserted that these were "diminishing returns" industries: autonomous technological progress or increasing capital investment may conceal this characteristic, but they do not remove its significance. In some of the countries, the relatively higher productivity growth rate in agriculture associated with a fast overall rate of growth may simply reflect the absorption of surplus labor into secondary and tertiary occupations, and is not necessarily (or not fully) the result of technological progress in the proper sense nor of increased capital investment per unit of output.

There remains the tertiary sector, comprising the many different kinds of services which together account for 40 to 50 percent or more of the total output and employment of the advanced countries. Throughout a considerable part of this sector "productivity" is a meaningless notion, since "output" cannot be measured independently of "input." In areas, such as hairdressing, catering, or laundries, where output could, in principle, be measured independently, economies of scale, internal or external, are not likely to play an important role. In yet other fields, such as distribution, the growth of *total* output is merely a reflection of the rate of growth of commodity production. The rate of increase of productivity, provided that excess capacity exists, will in this case vary in automatic response to the rate of growth of production in the primary and secondary sectors, and the consequent growth in consumption. It is just as easy to sell two packages of cigarettes to a customer in a shop as one package. This is not meant, of course, to deny that large-scale methods of distribution are superior to small-scale methods, or to minimize the importance of labor-saving innovations, for example, the supermarkets. But the productivity growth resulting from such changes in techniques is not dependent on the rate of growth of aggregate demand: the productivity growth could equally well take place irrespective of whether the total turnover of the distributive sector rises fast or slowly.

To sum up, then, the dominant influence on the rate of economic growth seems to be the growth rate of manufacturing output (together with the ancillary activities, public utilities, and construction). This is so not only because the growth rate of productivity in the industrial sector itself rises but also because the growth rate will tend to increase the rate of productivity growth in the other sectors. This may happen both in agriculture and in the distributive trades, partly on account of the absorption of surplus labor and partly because of a faster increase in the flow of goods into consumption. But, more generally, industrialization tends to accelerate the rate of change of technology, not just in one sector, but in the economy as a whole.

We still need to ask, however, why some countries have managed to increase their rate of manufacturing production so much faster than others. I shall analyze the nature of these influences in the second lecture.

LECTURE II

Advanced Countries

and Mature Economies

AS ALLYN YOUNG emphasized in his paper to which I have already referred, in order that there should be self-sustained growth, two conditions must be present: *returns* must increase, and the demand for commodities must be *elastic*. He defined the latter condition "in the special sense that a small increase in its supply will be attended by an increase in the amounts of other commodities which can be had in exchange for it. Under such conditions an increase in the supply of one commodity *is* an increase in the demand for other commodities, and it must be supposed that every increase in demand will evoke an increase in supply."[1]

This description emphasizes the nature of growth in the economic process as the result of a complex

---

[1] Young, "Increasing Returns and Economic Progress," *Economic Journal,* December 1928, p. 534.

process of interaction between demand increases which have been induced by increases in supply, and increases in supply caused by increases in demand. When we look at the market as a whole—i.e., view its economic mechanism as a whole, whether it is an isolated economy or the world economy as a unit— goods are exchanged against goods. An increase in demand for one commodity, or group of commodities, reflects the increased supply of something else: an increase in the supply of commodities is the cause of increased demand for commodities. The process of growth is thus the result of a chain reaction, the nature of which is conditioned both by demand elasticities and supply constraints. The former will depend partly on the manner in which individuals, in their capacity as consumers, allocate any increase in income between different goods and services; partly on the manner in which producers respond by increasing investment to increases in demand. This, again, depends on psychological as well as on technological factors. The speed of the chain reaction will be greater, the truer it is that consumers choose to buy more of those goods with a large supply response and the larger the response on the demand side caused by increases in production. The purpose of my lecture today is to view this process from a particular angle: to consider why it is that the manufacturing output of some countries rises so much faster than that of others. It will be convenient, if only for expository purposes, to look at the matter in two stages: first, from the point of view of the sources of demand; and, second, from the point of view of the factors which govern potential supply.

Looking at the problem from the demand side first, we have three main sources of demand: consumption; domestic investment; and net exports, that is, the net excess of exports over imports. One could add a fourth, demand originating in the government's current expenditures on manufactures, but apart from special circumstances such as a period of rapidly growing armament expenditures, government is not likely to play an important autonomous role in the growth of demand.

As far as personal consumption is concerned, there is a familiar relation between the level of real income and the structure of consumer demand. At low levels of income, a high proportion both of average and of marginal income is devoted to food. In an intermediate zone of real income per capita, the income elasticity of demand for manufactured goods is high; that is to say, a growing proportion of total consumers' expenditure is spent on manufactured goods. At still higher levels of real income per capita, the income elasticity of demand for manufactures tails off both absolutely and relative to demand for services. Were it not for the continued appearance of new commodities, such as washing machines or vacuum cleaners, which provide substitutes for services, the elasticity of demand at these higher levels would fall off more rapidly. In the intermediate zone, where the proportion spent on manufactures is both large and growing, there is a two-way relationship conducive to fast economic growth. The expansion of the industrial sector stimulates the rate of growth of real incomes, and the rise in real income itself increases the growth rate of demand for industrial output.

But this is not all. An even more important source of growth in demand is capital investment. Once a country attains that level of industrialization at which it can satisfy its own needs, not just in consumption goods, but in plant and machinery as well, the stage is set for a faster rate of growth of the manufacturing sector. For in these circumstances the manufacturing sector generates demand for its own products in the very process of supplying them. The expansion of capacity in the investment goods sector feeds upon itself, by increasing the growth rate of demand for its own output, thereby providing both the incentives and the means for its own further expansion. The establishment of an investment goods sector thus provides for a built-in element of acceleration in the rate of growth of demand for manufactured goods. If entrepreneurs are confident and optimistic about continued expansion, and if the expansion of output is not held up by shortages of basic raw materials, this acceleration would continue up to the limit imposed by technological constraints, i.e. the input/output relationships *within* the investment goods sector itself.

The third source of the rate of growth of demand resides in the changing structure of foreign trade, that is, the behavior of imports and exports. When a country starts to industrialize, its imports of manufactured consumer goods tend to diminish while its imports of machinery and equipment increase. During this phase, the growth rate of demand for domestic manufactures—which, at that stage, generally consist of the so-called "light industries," primarily textiles—rises more rapidly than total consumption on account of the substitution of home production for imports. But as the experience of many countries has shown, the stimulus to industrialization afforded by this peters out as the process of "import substitution" is gradually completed. To maintain development, it is necessary for the industrializing country to enter a second stage during which it becomes a growing net exporter of manufactured consumer goods. A further stage of industrialization can be identified in which the country engages in "import substitution" in the sphere of capital goods. Historically this stage may overlap with the second stage. We have already discussed the reasons for expecting it to be associated with a fast growth rate because, during this third stage, "heavy industries" are growing out of relation to the growth of the rest of the economy. Finally, for the really successful developer, there is a fourth stage, in which the country becomes a growing net exporter of capital goods. It is at this stage that we are likely to find "explosive growth," when a fast rate of growth of external demand for the output of the heavy industries combines with the self-generated growth of demand which their own expansion has caused. I think it has been Japan's entry into this fourth stage of industrialization which has been mainly responsible for her phenomenally high postwar growth rate. Fast though her growth of consumption of manufactured goods has been, the growth due to the rise in output of engineering goods, both for domestic use and for exports, has been much greater. But this again is likely to be a transitional phenomenon: once a country has a fully developed capital goods sector, and once she has acquired a reasonable share of world trade in investment goods, the growth of demand for her manufactured output is bound to slow down, as the broad historical experience of the older industrialized countries has shown.

So far we have been viewing the problem from the demand side alone. At any of the stages considered, however, the actual course of development may be slowed down, or altogether interrupted, by supply constraints. In fact, for reasons explained later on, it is inevitable that sooner or later the rate of growth should be slowed down because of supply constraints, even if the fast rate of growth of demand could be maintained.

Such supply constraints can be in one of two areas or both: commodities and/or labor. As the industrial sector expands, it absorbs a growing amount of goods and services produced outside the industrial sector: these may be the products of agriculture or mining (food and industrial materials), or manufactures which it does not provide itself, or not in sufficient quantities, and which have to be imported. The latter factor is relatively more important in the earlier stages of development. Yet, as recent experience has shown, there is plenty of scope, even among the industrially highly developed countries, for trade in manufactured goods for industrial use, both finished goods and components. Further, industrial growth generates demand for many kinds of services —banking, insurance and professional services of various kinds—and is thus partly responsible for a fast expansion of the "tertiary sector."

If we look at a single country, and not the industrialized countries as a group, a commodity constraint takes the form of a balance of payments constraint. It comes about because, at the given growth rate, imports increase faster than exports. This is specially likely to happen in the early stages of industrialization when, despite import substitution, there is considerable need for increased imports, yet the growth of industry at that time adds little or

33

nothing to the country's export potential. It has also been suggested that, for rather different reasons, a commodity constraint in the form of a balance of payments constraint may also slow down the rate of growth of industrially advanced countries; and it is a widely held view that it has been a major factor in limiting the rate of economic growth of postwar Britain and, to a lesser extent, of the United States. I shall come back to this later.

The other major supply constraint is not savings nor investment, but manpower. It is perfectly true that a higher rate of growth of capital is an essential condition of a higher rate of growth of output and, generally, though not, according to the figures, invariably, it requires a higher share of investment in output and hence a higher share of savings in income. But this does not mean that a shortage of savings is likely to be a bottleneck for the development of the industrial sector, except, perhaps, in the sense that a balance of payments constraint could, in some situations, reflect a genuine shortage of savings. In advanced industrial countries, however, the savings that are necessary for a higher rate of growth of capital are self-generated by the production process: most, if not all, of the finance for expansion comes out of undistributed profits. In cases of a higher rate of growth of output, profits are invariably higher as a share of income, and they invariably rise faster. Investment rises in response to a higher utilization of existing capacity; both profits and savings rise *pari passu* with the rise in investment.

With regard to manpower, the position is rather different. For although a higher growth rate of manufacturing output induces an increased growth rate of productivity, this productivity increase is not sufficient in itself to obviate the need for a faster growth of manpower. Increased productivity provides only one-half of the additional resources required; we still need increased employment for the other half.

Historical evidence fully supports the view that a fast rate of industrial growth is always accompanied by a fast rate of growth of employment in both the secondary and tertiary sectors. The main source of this labor is not the growth of population so much, nor even immigration, but the reservoir of surplus labor, the "disguised unemployment," on the land. As a country becomes more industrialized, there is a steady transfer of labor from rural to urban areas, and the percentage of the labor force engaged in agriculture falls dramatically. But the longer the process goes on, the smaller the agricultural labor force remaining, the smaller is the percentage addition to the labor force in the secondary and tertiary sectors that accrues from this source. At the same time, the incentives for the movement of labor become weaker as the gap between agricultural and industrial production, and the differences in the level

35

of earnings, are gradually eliminated. Table 3 shows the rate of growth in the total labor force, and the rate of change in employment in the primary, secondary, and tertiary occupations, and Table 4 shows

Table 3. Rates of Growth of Labor Force, and the Rate of Change of Employment in Agriculture, Mining, Industry, and Services.

			Twelve Countries 1954–64		
	Rate of Growth of Labor Force	*Rate of Growth of Employment* in Agriculture and Mining*	*Rate of Growth of Employment† in Industry and Services*		
			Total	*Industry*	*Services*
Japan	1.5	–2.6	5.4	5.8	5.1
Italy	–0.1	–4.5	3.9	4.4	3.2
W. Germany	1.4‡	–4.1‡	2.8‡	2.7‡	2.9‡
Austria	0.2§	–3.6§	2.3	2.0	2.6
France	0.2	–3.5	2.2	1.9	2.4
Denmark	0.8||	–2.8||	2.2||	2.5||	1.9||
Netherlands	1.3	–2.0	2.3	1.9	2.7
Belgium	0.3	–4.4	1.9	1.5	2.3
Norway	0.3	–2.5	1.3	0.5	2.0
Canada	2.3	–2.8	3.5	2.3	4.3
U.K.	0.6	–2.3	1.1	0.6	1.6
U.S.	1.3	–2.4	1.8	0.8	2.4

Source: O.E.C.D. Manpower Statistics.
*Including Self-Employed and Unpaid Family Workers
†Wage and Salary Earners
‡1957–64
§1951–63
||1955–64

the percentage composition of the labor force in 1962–1963 as between the three sectors.

One of the remarkable features of Table 3 is the similarity between the countries in the rates of fall of employment in agriculture and mining: in all countries it varied between $2\frac{1}{2}$ and $4\frac{1}{2}$ percent a year. But in countries where the agricultural labor force was still large as a percentage of the total labor force, this meant a *substantial* annual addition to the labor force in industry and services, both absolutely and in relation to the rate of growth of the total labor force. The latter was relatively small in most countries. In countries with a relatively small primary sector, such as the U.S. and the U.K., the rate of increase of manpower in the secondary and tertiary sectors was very much less.

We can also see from Table 3 that the absorption of labor into services was very substantial in all countries: but, although in the fast-growing countries it tended to lag behind the rate of growth of labor in the industrial sector, in the slow-growing countries it was the other way round. Thus, in these latter countries, the increase of employment in the tertiary sector greatly exceeded the increase in employment in industry. This may have reflected the fact that the growth in labor requirements in services proved less sensitive to changes in the rate of economic growth than the growth of labor requirements in industry. For example, the expansion of educational and health services tends to go in much the same way, irrespective of whether commodity output rises fast or slowly. But it is also possible that the relatively large increase in service employment in the slow-growing countries was itself a reflection of lack of demand, or the instability of demand, for labor in manufacturing. As far as Britain is concerned, it may have been a by-product of the stop-go cycle: there may have been a drift of labor into services as a result of the fall in employment in manufacturing in the "stop" phase which was not, or not sufficiently, reversed in the subsequent "go" phase.

In the United States, on the other hand, the slow rate of growth of demand for labor in the industrial sector in the last forty years or so may itself have contributed to the relatively large increase in employment in services. If we compared the position in 1920 with 1963, the share of the labor force in the tertiary sector increased from 40 percent to 60 percent. This was balanced by a small fall in the share of industry (by around 2 percent) and a large fall in the share of agriculture from 26 percent in 1920 to just over 8 percent in 1960.

The commonly accepted explanation of this is two-fold. The first aspect is the high-income elasticity of demand for services at the level of real income attained in the United States after the first world war. Services included in this case are those provided through the market mechanism, such as hotels or places of entertainment, and those services which are communally provided such as health and education. The second aspect is the slower rate of growth of productivity in the services sector, relative to the manufacturing sector. It is understood from this fact that a given rate of increase in the volume of real output in services (with all the qualifications about the meaning, or measurement of "real" output in services), requires a proportionately higher rate of increase in labor input.

Recent studies have cast doubt on the assumption of a high-income elasticity of demand for services[2] and suggest that this elasticity is barely above unity. The disproportionate growth in service employments is attributed, not to the changing structure of demand, but to the relatively low rate of productivity growth in service industries in comparison with both primary and secondary production. Yet I wonder whether this explanation goes to the heart of the matter. If the demand for labor in services increased faster than in the rest of the economy, and if the movement of labor into service industries were in response to this, one would expect wages in the service industries to rise faster than in the rest of the economy in order to attract the required labor. As far as I can judge, this has not happened. The rise

---

[2]For example, Victor R. Fuchs, *The Growing Importance of the Service Industries* (New York: National Bureau of Economic Research, Occasional Paper, No. 96, 1965).

in earnings per employee in manufacturing industries has been faster than in services; the level of income per capita in services is only about 80 percent of the corresponding figure in the industrial sector. This is sometimes explained by a relatively larger amount of capital per worker in industry; but if this were the true explanation, one would expect it to be reflected in a higher share of gross profits in net output. Nor, I believe, could one account for it by the hypothesis that manufacturing makes a proportionately greater use of skilled or qualified manpower. Much the greater part of highly qualified manpower is employed in "services" of certain kinds rather than in industry.

It is possible, therefore, that at least some of the increase in services employment in the United States was not a true response to influences emanating from the side of demand but merely the passive consequence of the limited growth of employment opportunities in the industrial sector. The opportunities for increased employment through "work-sharing" of some kind—through the establishment of competing units which merely divide a given volume of business between them—are obviously much greater in the services sector than in industry. This is so because the average size of the individual firm or establishment is so much smaller, and entry into the market is so much easier in services than in manufacturing. In addition, price competition is less prominent. As John Stuart Mill observed as early as 1848, competition in distribution and in professions "often operates not by lowering prices, but merely by dividing the gains of the high price among a greater number of dealers."[3] If this is true, and if earnings in service employments are below those in industry, a faster rate of growth in the demand for labor in industry would automatically attract labor from the services sector and thereby secure the additional manpower required for sustaining a faster rate of growth of output. But this means that, although the statistics on the distribution of manpower shown in Table 3 suggest that the United States is approaching the same kind of situation of manpower shortage as the United Kingdom, in reality the position of the two countries is rather different. While the absorption of labor in services has also been disproportionately large in Britain, the rise in incomes per capita in the tertiary sector has been just as large as in the rest of the economy; in the United Kingdom, unlike the United States, incomes per capita in services are nearly as large as in industry. In the United Kingdom when the growth of manufacturing ouput grinds to a halt because of a shortage of labor, the manufacturing sector is not capable of drawing labor from services since earnings in the two sectors are nearly the same. Inelasticity in the supply of labor seems to me the main constraint limiting the growth poten-

[3]*Principles of Political Economy,* Book II, Chapter IV, Sec. 3.

tial of the United Kingdom in a way in which it is not true of any other advanced country, with the possible exception of Germany in the last few years.

I should like to end this lecture with a more detailed comparison of the position of our two countries, the United States and the United Kingdom. As we have seen, the performance of the two countries in the 1950's was very similar; they were both slow growers. But as subsequent events have shown, the *causes* of slow growth were rather different in the two countries. The U.S. suffered from the pre-war disease of an insufficiency in effective demand. There was plenty of unemployment, both open and disguised: an orthodox Keynesian situation calling for Keynesian remedies. *Anything* that increased the growth of effective demand for manufactures was bound to step up the rate of growth of productivity, both in manufactures and also in the rest of the economy. Of course, a faster rate of economic growth was bound to entail a faster growth of imports, and hence required a faster rate of growth of exports to sustain it, if growing balance of payments deficits were to be avoided. The very fact of a faster growth of output, however, could be expected to act as a stimulus to exports; when output and capacity are both enlarged, productivity is increased and unit costs are reduced. It is then easier to sell more abroad. But, clearly, an export-led increase in demand would make it far easier to sustain a higher growth rate than one which relies on stimulating home demand through fiscal measures. In that sense there is some truth in the assertion that the U.S. has suffered, and possibly still suffers, from a balance of payments constraint. If the foreign demand for U.S. goods had increased faster, the country could have combined a higher rate of growth with a stronger balance of payments.

But when this same diagnosis is applied to the United Kingdom, I am less sure of its validity. It is certainly true that brief periods of relatively fast growth during the last twenty years were invariably attended by a rapid growth of imports, resulting in balance of payments deficits. It was the occurrence of these deficits, as much as the labor shortages and the resulting inflation, which forced the introduction of sharp counterinflationary measures which brought these periods to an end. It is equally true that if the trend rate of growth of her exports had been higher Britain could have sustained higher rates of growth of imports, and that if the rhythm of our development had been more even, imports would not have risen as fast as they did during the recovery phases (since this was much under the influence of the stockbuilding cycle).

All this does not necessarily prove that the balance of payments was the *effective* constraint on the rate of economic growth of the U.K. This would only follow if it could also be shown that, with a faster rate of growth of exports, the country could have achieved a higher rate of growth of manufacturing production, or else that the U.K. could have increased exports at a faster rate while keeping domestic investment and consumption rising at a lower rate. In the latter context it must be remembered that the volume of British exports has been pretty large, around 30 percent, in relation to the total volume of manufacturing production, and, although the share of her exports in world trade declined dramatically, the share of exports in total manufacturing output remained remarkably steady. It is possible to interpret this by saying that it was the trend rate of growth of exports which governed the trend rate of growth of production, since any higher rate of growth of production would not, over a run of years, have been compatible with keeping the balance of payments even. It is also possible to interpret this in the opposite way: over a run of years it was the rate of growth of production of exportable goods which determined the rate of growth of British exports.

The important question is whether, *apart* from balance of payments constraints, it would have been possible to increase U.K. manufacturing output at a faster rate. Was the growth in production mainly governed by the growth in demand for manufactured products, or was it governed by supply constraints, which would have frustrated a higher growth of output, irrespective of the growth in demand?

Advanced Countries: Mature Economies

And here we come back to the labor situation. In postwar Britain, periods of rapid growth in manufacturing industry invariably led to severe labor shortages which slowed down the growth of output and which continued for some time after production reached its cyclical peak. In fact, on almost every occasion, employment continued to rise after output had begun to fall. All this suggests that a higher rate of growth could not have been maintained unless more manpower had been made available to the manufacturing industry. Lacking "backward" sectors of low earnings, it is not easy to see where this manpower could have come from. Moreover, the situation grew worse with the passage of years. That is, the rate of growth of employment in manufacturing industry slowed down more in each successive cycle of the postwar period.

In the U.S., the position is fundamentally different. Despite the very rapid fall in the agricultural labor force, incomes per capita in agriculture are still only around one-half the national average, which suggests that there is still plenty of scope for productivity increases in agriculture ensuing from, or associated with, the continued transference of labor from rural to urban occupations. For the reasons already explained, the U.S. may also possess a considerable labor reserve in the tertiary sector. In addition, the rate of growth of the working population is in itself relatively large, and, based on present

45

demographic projections, it is likely to remain so. For all these reasons I cannot see that the growth potential of the United States is likely to be constrained in the near future by labor bottlenecks. Provided that a balance of payments constraint can be avoided through an adequate rate of growth of exports, I can see no compelling reason why the recent G.N.P. growth rate of around 4.5 percent could not be sustained for many years ahead.

There is an important difference between the notion of an "advanced country"—which is generally understood to mean a country with a high level of productivity and of income-per-capita—and the notion of a "mature economy," which relates to an economy in which sectoral differences in output-per-capita and in the level of earnings have largely been eliminated. Though most industrialized countries are "advanced countries" in the above sense, only a few of them have reached the degree of industrialization at which the supply of labor to industry ceases to be elastic—in other words, the stage in which an increase in the demand for labor by the industrial sector fails to elicit a response in terms of an accelerated transfer of labor from the low-productivity sectors. Britain, having started the process of industrialization earlier than any other country, has reached "maturity" earlier; almost alone among "advanced countries," she has attained the distribution of the labor force between agriculture, industry,

and services at which output-per-capita in both agriculture and services is as high, or almost as high, as
in manufacturing. There are disadvantages of an
early start, as well as advantages, as is shown by the
fact that some of the latecomers to industrialization
have attained higher levels of industrial efficiency
even before they became fully industrialized.

Ultimately, if the basic analysis put forward in
these lectures is correct, *all* countries will approach
the same situation which now faces the United Kingdom in which the shortage of labor becomes the
main constraint limiting economic growth. As the
figures in Table 4 show, a number of important
countries, such as Japan, Italy, and France, with an
agricultural labor force of 20 to 30 percent, have a
considerable period of potentially fast growth ahead
of them; others, such as Germany and Belgium, are
more closely approaching the structural pattern of
the United Kingdom.

Does that mean that as more and more countries
attain the state of "maturity" the rate of growth of
the world economy is bound to slow down? Ultimately, perhaps, the answer is yes; but that day may
be a long way off. For one thing, there is plenty of
scope, as will be argued in the next lecture, for
accelerated growth in the present underdeveloped,
or "low income," countries which could more than
compensate for any slowdown of growth among the
advanced countries. For another thing, the group

47

Table 4. Percentage Composition of Total Employment Between Primary, Secondary, and Tertiary Occupations.

Twelve Countries, 1962–63 average (in percentages)

	PRIMARY	SECONDARY	TERTIARY	
	(Agriculture and Mining)	*(Manufacturing, Construction & Public Utilities)*	*(Services)**	*Total*
Japan	30.0	30.3	39.7	100
Italy	27.8	39.4	32.8	100
Austria†	23.8	40.6	35.6	100
France	21.1	37.0	41.9	100
Norway	20.8	33.8	44.5	100
Denmark	19.1	39.5	41.4	100
West Germany	14.3	42.6	39.5	100
Canada	12.9	32.7	54.4	100
Netherlands	12.0	42.3	45.7	100
Belgium	9.4	40.6	48.2	100
U.S.	8.9	30.7	60.4	100
U.K.	6.7	44.0	49.3	100

Source: O.E.C.D. Manpower Statistics.

*Includes Transport, Distribution, Financial and other Services, Public Administration, etc.

†1961.

of advanced countries themselves could postpone the consequences of approaching "maturity" by inter-twining their economies more closely. Precisely because economies of scale in industry are the main engine of fast growth, there is plenty of scope for fast rates of progress through greater international specialization, attained through an intensification of trade. If each country concentrated its industrial production in fewer fields and obtained more of its own requirements from others, this could accelerate productivity growth in much the same way as in the case when a higher rate of growth of industrial production is spread over the whole field.

LECTURE III

Problems of Industrialization

in Underdeveloped Countries

THIS LAST LECTURE I should like to devote to the problems of the underdeveloped countries. Why is it that they have remained so far behind; why did they fail to participate in the prolonged process of fast growth associated with the rise of modern capitalism? And what are the main obstacles which limit their growth rates today? These questions, of course, are far more important, and far more intriguing, than the questions of the differences of growth rates among the advanced countries which I have discussed so far. They are also far more difficult, since they involve issues of sociology and social anthropology. These issues are not only beyond my own competence but, I am tempted to say, beyond the present reach of these disciplines themselves—at least if one is looking for scientific hypotheses that purport to establish quantifiable relationships that

53

are capable of being tested. Questions such as why the process of fast growth did not extend to Spain or the Spanish colonies in the last 100 years, or why it should have occurred in Japan and failed to occur in the other areas of South-East Asia are not fully answerable in terms of economics. They involve a general theory of social and cultural development which cannot, as yet, be said to exist.

Confining ourselves to economics, the question to be asked is: what were the factors which prevented or hampered the industrialization of these countries? For there can be little doubt that the kind of economic growth which involves the use of modern technology and which eventuates in high real income per capita, is inconceivable without industrialization. In that sense there are no alternative roads to economic development. The reason for this is not only, or mainly, because, as real income rises, only a diminishing proportion of income is spent on food, and a growing proportion is spent on industrial products and services. One could conceive of a country "specializing" entirely in agriculture and obtaining all its industrial requirements from abroad. But it could never become a high income country simply because high-productivity agriculture could never absorb more than a fraction of the working population on the available land. The best proof of this is found in the fact that those advanced countries which have "specialized" in exporting agricultural products and importing manufactured goods, such as Australia, New Zealand, and Denmark, have, nevertheless, only a low proportion of their labor force in agriculture, not only absolutely, but relatively to industry.

The question then is, what hampered, or prevented, the process of industrialization outside a favored group of countries? In any particular historical case, one could probably point to quite a number of factors. But if one is looking for some *general* cause which is common to most countries, including the relatively underpopulated regions of Latin America and the overpopulated regions of South-East Asia, it is the backwardness and stagnation of agriculture. The growth of the secondary and tertiary sectors is dependent on the growth of the "agricultural surplus," that is, the excess of food production over the food consumption of the food producers themselves. This aspect of development was first emphasized by Adam Smith.

The importance of the agricultural surplus has two main aspects. In the first place, the rate at which non-agricultural employment can increase depends on the rate of growth of *marketed* food supplies. Food is the "wage good" par excellence, and any attempt to increase urban employment at a faster rate than the agricultural surplus permits, is bound, sooner or later, to be vitiated through violent inflation. Indeed, the ratio of agricultural production to the self-consumption in the agricultural sector, which is invariably low in countries where agriculture is backward, is perhaps the best available indicator of the "development potential" of an economy.

In the second place, the growth of the agricultural surplus is an essential condition for providing the growth of *purchasing power* necessary for sustaining industrial expansion. The increase in the demand for manufactured products cannot be wholly self-generated; it depends on the increase in the supply of other things for which the products of industry are exchanged. These other things are mainly the products of agriculture, which, as we have seen, is *not* subject to increasing returns. This means that, whereas the growth of industrial production is primarily governed by the growth of effective demand, in the growth of agricultural production (in the early stages of development, at any rate), the element of *response* to outside stimuli plays a much smaller role. Agricultural production has an autonomous momentum which is mainly dependent on the progress of land-saving, as distinct from labor-saving, innovations. These land-saving innovations include not only technical discoveries but the social framework of agriculture, the whole network of institutions which determine land tenure, and the progress of education in rural areas. The emergence of a progressive agriculture was the key to the progress of industrialization in Europe. It is no accident that in

England, as elsewhere in Europe, the so-called "agricultural revolution" historically preceded the "industrial revolution." In some countries, as in England, this was brought about by the landlords expropriating the hereditary tenants; in others, as in France, by the hereditary tenants expropriating the landlords. Land reform, with the consequent agricultural revolution, has also played a vital role in the development of Japan after the Meiji Restoration. In countries where this "agricultural revolution" failed to occur—whether owing to the vestigal survival of feudalism, as in the Spanish ex-colonies, or to the ancient forms of land tenure, as in India—industrial development could never get started. Even when, for reasons that I shall proceed to explain, it *did* get started, it could not be long sustained.

The initial stimulus to development of most, though not all, backward countries came from the growth of exports of the products of plantation agriculture or mining. With the growth of industry in Europe, markets were created for temperate foodstuffs, tropical products, and minerals. The exploitation of these opportunities sometimes proceeded on the initiative of native producers, but more frequently through European capital or enterprise. It is often contended that the growth of foreign-controlled mines and plantations was a "foreign enclave" which contributed little to the economic growth of the countries in which these developments occurred. This is not wholly accurate. It brought with it the educational stimulus of foreign contacts; and, what is more important, it was a source of export earnings which could be channelled, in a suitable political environment, to provide within limits the means for developing local industries.

The development of local industries in these areas also depended, however, on the adoption of protective tariffs. In the absence of these, the high initial costs, in terms of agricultural products, of home-produced manufactured goods imposed too severe a handicap on any latecomer to industrialization to make manufacturing activities commercially profitable. The advantage of any underdeveloped country in the industrial field resides in low wages. In the initial stages of industrialization this advantage is more than offset by low productivity. Hence, under conditions of free trade, when the domestic price of manufactures is determined by world prices, domestic production may not get started.

When the subsidy to "infant industries" takes the form of a protective tariff, however, the internal *price* structure is adapted to the internal *cost* structure; not the *internal* cost structure to the *external* price structure. Industries are developed on the basis of a price relationship between manufactured goods and primary products, which is divorced from the prevailing world price relationship. Import duties are efficacious in promoting industrialization so long as there is scope for creating an internal demand for home-produced manufactured goods which *substitutes* for imports. But once the limits of import substitution have been reached, the momentum for further industrialization is pretty well exhausted; further growth of domestic industry is dependent on the growth of internal purchasing power, which is ultimately governed by the growth of production in the complementary sector of the economy, which is agriculture.

This course of events is illustrated by the history of many Latin American countries. Countries such as Chile, Argentine, and Brazil each went through a phase of rapid growth following the establishment of highly protective tariffs or import prohibitions during the Great Depression. But in each case this phase was followed by a prolonged period of very slow growth, or stagnation, combined with prolonged and violent inflation.

I think the basic explanation for this result is that the phase of industrialization involved the rapid growth of non-agricultural employment, and hence a rapid increase in the demand for food supplies. But the agricultural sector failed to respond to the stimulus in an adequate manner. At the same time, the growth of the economy, and the process of industrialization itself, raised import requirements while adding little, if anything, to export capacity, thus inducing a chronic balance of payments problem.[1] The latter made it difficult, if not impossible, to make good the deficiency in food supplies through imports. There emerged, therefore, a steady upward pressure on food prices which made inevitable, sooner or later, a compensatory rise in money wages. The periodic rise in money wages converted the process into a spiral inflation. To stop this inflation would have entailed a sufficient rise in food prices in terms of wages, or in terms of industrial products, to eliminate the excess demand for food. This was impossible politically, and would probably have entailed large reductions in the volume of urban employment.

The countries in Latin America which have avoided these large and long-continuing inflations have been those which succeeded in raising the productivity of domestic agriculture or those which succeeded in increasing their export earnings fast enough to allow the relatively free importation of food and other necessities. Mexico, an example of the first, raised domestic agricultural productivity following the land reforms of the 1930's; Venezuela and Peru

---

[1] It may sound paradoxical that industrialization arising out of "import substitution" should cause a *rise* in import requirements. The main explanation is that the process increased the *volume* of the G.N.P. and this, as such, tends to raise total imports, even when the industrialization process succeeds in reducing the *propensity* to import, that is, the proportion of imports to the G.N.P. Also, there are added import requirements connected with investment.

are two which succeeded in the latter course. Monetary and fiscal policies had very little to do with the occurrence or persistence of these inflations. Western economists were slow to recognize this point, with the result that the stabilization policies repeatedly urged by international organizations proved abortive in halting these inflations, though they frequently involved contractions in the level of production and employment.

The main lesson is that it is impossible for a country, unless it be of an exceptional size and extremely well endowed with natural resources of all kinds, to pass through successive phases of economic development, except when it succeeds in raising its export potential *pari passu* with the growth of domestic output. Bismarck's famous statement "We must export or die!" showed that he thoroughly understood the theories of Friedrich List. List, the original advocate of industrialization through protection, put it forward as "an infant industry" argument. Industries, he said, need protection in their "infancy"; once they grow to a certain size, and become well-established, the protection should be withdrawn, or the industries will fail to become competitive in export markets. But this assumes that the size of the internal market is sufficiently large to enable productivity to rise to the point at which costs, given the level of domestic wages, become sufficiently low to be competitive with world prices.

It is no accident that the cotton textile industry represents the one example in which a series of developing countries succeeded in attaining a strong competitive position in world markets. It is an industry which caters for mass requirements and in which, therefore, the size of the domestic market, even in low income countries, is relatively large. It is also an industry in which modern techniques and know-how are relatively easily acquired and economies of large scale cease to be significant beyond a certain stage. In most other cases, the establishment of the domestic industry fails to increase the capacity to export simply because costs, expressed in terms of a common currency (local costs converted to dollar costs at the prevailing rates of exchange) remain too high.

It is important to emphasize that this defect does not reflect too high exchange rates and cannot be remedied by devaluation. Industrial costs are too high not just in terms of international currencies but in relation to the prices of primary products. They are too high precisely because they are dependent on an internal system of prices which is divorced from world prices. A change in the exchange rate cannot cure this situation. The exchange rate which would make it possible for an underdeveloped country to develop export markets in manufactured products would mean a considerable undervaluation of its currency in terms of primary products. Inevitably, an inflation of domestic costs and prices is thereby generated that soon neutralizes any beneficial effect of the change in the exchange rate on the export costs of manufacturers. This is the reason why frequent attempts to cure the balance of payments deficits of underdeveloped countries through devaluation—the introduction of "more realistic" exchange rates—generally has proved abortive. The effect of the change in the exchange rate has almost invariably been cancelled, within a brief period, by the resulting extra bout of domestic inflation.

This problem would not have arisen if the establishment of domestic industries had proceeded by means of direct subsidies instead of protective tariffs. This was the case, I believe, in Japan which, consequently, succeeded in developing an export potential at an early stage of industrial development. But this was only because Japan possessed a fiscal system capable of raising large sums in direct taxes which were imposed on the agricultural sector. Most other countries chose the easier path of taxing the agricultural sector indirectly through the deterioration of the internal terms of trade, which followed the imposition of import duties.

Failing a system of internal subsidies, the growth of an export potential could, nevertheless, be ensured if the imposition of import duties were balanced by equivalent export subsidies. For example, a commodity attracting an *ad valorem* import duty of 33½ percent should attract an export subsidy of 25 percent. This balancing would ensure, from the point of view of exports, much the same results as if the industry had been promoted by means of internal subsidies instead of import duties. At the same time, it would not raise the same problem in terms of public revenue and expenditure. At the beginning, the import duties would yield more revenue than the cost of the subsidies, and by the time they come to involve a net cost, when exports begin to exceed imports, the budgetary problem of financing this may not loom so large.

It would be wrong to give the impression, however, that all that underdeveloped countries need to do in order to remove the main impediments to their continued industrialization and development is to make sure that any protection to domestic industries by way of import duties or other types of import restriction is balanced by equivalent export subsidies. The main obstacle to growing industrial exports from low-wage countries is not so much the difficulty of providing them but the reluctance of the high-income countries to accept them. Although one underdeveloped country can develop trade with another underdeveloped country, all are ultimately dependent on the import of commodities of numerous kinds which only the developed countries can provide. Hence, it is essential for them to increase their exports at a satisfactory rate to the advanced countries. But this cannot be achieved through the exports of primary commodities alone because the demand for them is not only limited but is increasing at a moderate rate and has been projected to increase in the next twenty years or so at no more than 3 to 4 percent a year. The economic development of the underdeveloped countries could only be successful, therefore, if they went through the same phases as the present advanced countries have gone through in the past, increasing progressively the volume and range of their industrial exports.

It is precisely here that the current commercial policies of the advanced countries pose an almost insurmountable obstacle. In that respect, the position of a current developer is much worse than that of the latecomers to industrialization in the 19th century. When the countries of Continental Europe and the Scandinavian countries began to develop their industrial exports, they did so under conditions of relatively free trade, at any rate, they faced no discrimination. Japan, which came into the world market later, paying wages which were much lower relative to the wages prevailing in the developed countries, faced far more serious obstacles. Nevertheless, since World War II, Japan has largely suceeded in overcoming them, which, in turn, has largely been due at the critical stage to the liberal policy of the United States in regard to Japanese imports. But this policy did not extend in the same way to other underdeveloped countries, and, at the moment, the industrial exports of India, Pakistan, Hong Kong, and other developing countries are confined by import quotas and other forms of trade discrimination.

All this is based on the mistaken premise that manufactured imports from a low-wage country impose a threat to the standard of living of the workers of high-wage countries. It can be easily shown that it is no more capable of imposing a threat than is technological progress, which results in the invention of substitute products of various kinds. Indeed, the effect of imports from low-wage countries on the real income of recipient countries is in no way different from the effect of labor-saving inventions of any kind. In either case, there is a threat to labor in a situation in which effective demand is static, so that the saving in labor will reduce employment rather than increase total production. And in either case there will be serious problems of adjustment and adaptation if the changes are too swift or sudden. But, whereas the adjustments connected with the progress of technology have come to be accepted as part of the cost of economic progress that can, and must, be taken in its stride, the entirely analogous adjustments necessitated by enlarged import opportunities are strongly resisted. In what way does the development of a textile industry in, say, Hong Kong, differ from the invention of synthetic fibre? Countries like the U.K. or the U.S. would never dream of putting an obstacle in the way of the exploitation of a new invention, however much it may threaten some old-established industry. Yet they are perfectly ready to invoke the escape clauses of the G.A.T.T. to protect their own textile industries from the threat of "market disruption."

This restriction on trade, I am convinced, is the major obstacle to the fast economic progress of the underdeveloped parts of the world, and one that is likely to become more serious as the differences in income levels between the advanced countries and the underdeveloped countries increase still further. I am not suggesting, of course, that historically the existence of the advanced industrial countries has hindered the development of the underdeveloped countries. On the contrary, the probability is that, in the absence of contacts with the developed countries which have produced large investments in the development of mining and plantation agriculture, the cultural and educational influences, and economic aid, the underdeveloped countries would be in very much the same state today that they were 100 or 200 years ago. But the fact remains that if they are to advance fast enough to raise their real incomes per capita to more reasonable levels, and to narrow the tremendous gap which now separates them from the advanced countries, they have no alternative except to engage in the same kind of process of fast industrialization which occurred in successive phases in

67

history in England, Western Europe, America, and Japan. In none of these instances, with the possible exception of the United States, could this development have taken place in the absence of a fast growth of industrial exports.

At this point the question might be raised: Suppose these commercial obstacles were progressively removed and suppose the underdeveloped countries, one by one, gradually attained the status of large industrial exporters, where would all this lead to? How would this tremendous volume of production and trade in industrial goods be absorbed, and how would the balance in the world production and consumption of foodstuffs, raw materials, and manufactured goods be preserved?

And this brings me to the last point which I should like to consider in these lectures. Suppose we do not focus our attention on any single country, developed or undeveloped—countries after all are political, social, or cultural entities, not economic ones—but consider the whole world economy as a unit? How fast can it develop, and what are the constraints on its rate of development? Is there such a thing as a growth potential for the world economy as a whole? And, if so, what determines it, and how is it related to the actual rate of growth?

Once we pose the question in this manner I think the answers suggest themselves quite naturally by the methods of our previous analysis. There can be no doubt that the world economy presents the picture of a vast underdeveloped area with certain "growth points" which are like the fast growing urban industrial areas of some of the underdeveloped countries, such as São Paulo in relation to Brazil. In the world context, these urban areas really encompass the whole of the developed countries, not just their own urban areas. The income differences between them and the underdeveloped countries are much larger than those between the industrial cities and the rural areas of underdeveloped countries. This, no doubt, is partly due to the existence of far greater limitations on the international mobility of labor. But the basic characteristics of the economic process are very much the same in the two cases.

The industrial areas produce manufactured goods and absorb foodstuffs and raw materials produced in the rural areas. The terms of trade between them fluctuate up and down as the growth in world manufacturing production causes the demand for primary products to run ahead of the growth in the supply of primary products, or vice versa. A great deal of the supply of primary products absorbed by the manufacturing sectors is either produced by the developed countries themselves, or is the result of past investment by the industrial countries in the underdeveloped countries. When the expansion of manufacturing production runs ahead of the growth in raw material supplies, the terms of trade move in favor of the primary producers. A period of high prices may lead to considerable new investment in the primary sector. This, in turn, is likely, at a later date, to accelerate the growth in primary products through the opening up of new producing areas, the expansion of existing facilities, and the acceleration of technological progress to improve varieties of crops, and so on. When these additional supplies eventually come to the market, primary product prices fall again; investment in primary production becomes less profitable. A prolonged period of low prices may set in before the rate of growth of supplies slows down sufficiently for the growth of demand to catch up again and restore prices to a remunerative level.

The rate of growth of world manufacturing production thus exerts a strong influence on the level of primary product prices and, in the longer run, on the rate of growth of primary production. But, with the market mechanism as it is, it cannot be asserted that there are any appreciable forces at work in the other direction to cause world manufacturing production to *expand* in response to increased availabilities of primary products. The fall in the prices of primary products should induce an acceleration in the rate of industrialization of the world. In fact, because of its adverse effect on the primary producers' export earnings and on the flow of international investment, the fall in the prices of primary products may tend to slow down the rate of industrial development, instead of accelerating it. The improvement in the terms of trade of the industrial countries, although it releases purchasing power which ought, in principle, to generate additional demand *within* the industrial sector, may actually have little net effect on the rate of growth of industrial countries. This can be said because any increase in demand emanating from *within* may be more than offset by reduced exports and reduced investment. It must be borne in mind that investment in the primary producing areas is normally also largely financed by the industrial countries; hence, the fall in the profitability of investment in primary products will tend to have adverse multiplier effects on the level of industrial activity.

The result is that the chain reaction of an increase in supply causing an increase in demand for other commodities, and thus, in turn, reacting on the demand for the first commodity, may not work, or not work as efficiently, as it could. In this case, one of the two conditions postulated by Allyn Young—that returns should increase and demands should be *elastic*—will not be satisfied. The limited elasticity of demand of the industrial countries for the products of the primary producing countries acts as a constraint which tends to slow down the rate of growth of the whole system. In these circumstances, increased industrialization in the less developed areas, provided it can be integrated with the world economy, is bound to accelerate the general rate of growth in both in the less developed areas and also the developed areas—in the latter at least up to the point when they become fully "mature" and their labor reserves are exhausted. As we have seen, most developed countries are far from having reached this position. There is, therefore, considerable scope for acceleration in the rate of growth of the world economy in all such situations in which the growth of marketable supplies of primary products is limited by the growth of demand for them, and not by supply constraints.

There is no doubt that, with the fast increase in the progress of technology in primary production, the rate of growth in world supplies of primary products could be stepped up if the existing demand constraints were removed. All the extra production in food and industrial materials could be absorbed through faster industrialization, provided only that the industrial products produced by the developing countries could be integrated into the stream of world trade in the same way as the manufactured goods produced by the developed countries. There is, therefore, tremendous scope for faster growth in the world economy, if only the existing obstacles to trade were removed, and if the advanced countries pursued monetary and fiscal policies which allowed a progressive elimination of import barriers while maintaining full employment.

Statistical Appendix

(a) The role of Manufacturing in Economic Growth

The significance of the relationship between the growth of manufacturing output and the growth of the G.D.P. shown in Table 1 has been tested (i) by reference to the relation of the growth of non-manufacturing output (i.e. G.D.P. *minus* G.D.P. in manufacturing) to the growth in manufacturing production; (ii) by relating the growth rate of G.D.P. to the *excess* of the growth rate of manufacturing production over the growth rate of the non-manufacturing sectors. The results are summarized in the following regression equations:[1]

(1) *Rate of growth of non-manufacturing output (Y) on rate of growth of manufacturing production (X)*

$$Y = 1.142 + 0.550X, R^2 = 0.824.$$
$$(0.080)$$

(2) *Rate of growth of G.D.P. (Y) on the excess of the rate of growth of manufacturing over the rate of growth of non-manufacturing production (X)*

$$Y = 3.351 + 0.954X, R^2 = 0.562.$$
$$(0.267)$$

Both of these are statistically significant at the 99 percent level and thus confirm the generalization derived from

[1]The four regression equations in this section relate to the same group of countries, and the same periods, as indicated in Table 1.

Appendix

Table 1. A comparison of regression (1) above with the regression in Table 1 shows that the exclusion of manufacturing output from G.D.P. makes no appreciable difference to the structural relationship: both the constants and the coefficients in the two equations are very similar.

The significance of these findings has been further tested by examining the relationship between the growth rate of G.D.P. and the growth rate of agricultural production, mining, and the output of services.[2] No correlation was found between the rate of growth of G.D.P. and the rate of growth of either agricultural production or mining. As between G.D.P. and G.D.P. originating in "services" there is a highly significant relationship but of a different character, as shown by the following equation:

(3) *Rate of growth of G.D.P. (Y) on rate of growth of G.D.P. in services (X)*

$$Y = -0.188 + 1.060X, R^2 = 0.930.$$
$$(0.092)$$

The fact that the coefficient is so near to unity, and the constant is negligible suggests that the causal relationship here is the other way round—i.e. that it is the rate of growth of G.D.P. which determines the rate of growth of the "output" of services. It also confirms recent American studies[3] referred to earlier which suggest that, contrary to general belief, the income-elasticity of demand for services is not significantly greater than unity; the fact that most countries

---

[2]The term "services" comprises transport and communications; wholesale and retail trade; banking, insurance and real estate; ownership of dwellings; public administration and defense; health and educational services and miscellaneous services.

[3]Cf. Victor R. Fuchs, *op. cit.*

Appendix

(as indicated in Table 3) had a higher rate of employment growth in "services" than in "industry" is not due to a high income-elasticity of demand, but to a lower rate of productivity growth in services. This latter finding is further confirmed by relating the rate of growth of output in "services" to the rate of growth of industrial production (manufacturing, construction, and public utilities):

(4) *Rate of growth of output in services (Y) on the rate of growth of industrial production (X)*

$$Y = 1.283 + 0.597X, R^2 = 0.846.$$
$$(0.0805)$$

This shows that the "real" output of services—as measured in the national accounts of each country at constant prices—grows less than in proportion to industrial output, even though employment grows (in most cases) more than in proportion.[4]

(b) The Verdoorn Law

The "Verdoorn Law" asserts that, with a higher rate of growth of output, both productivity and employment increase at a faster rate, the regression coefficients with respect to each being of the same order of magnitude. This relationship was also investigated with regard to other sectors of the economy for which comparable data could be found in the O.E.C.D. statistics—i.e. public utilities (gas, electricity, and water) and construction; agriculture and mining; transport and communications and "commerce" (the latter term

---

[4]The only exceptions in the period considered (i.e. 1953–54 to 1963–64—though this would not be true of the more recent period, 1960–65) were the U.S.A. and Canada, where the output of services grew at a somewhat higher rate than industrial output.

includes the distributive trades, banking, insurance and real estate).[5] Owing to the lack of data, some countries had to be omitted in some of the estimates, and a somewhat shorter period taken; also, it was not possible to adjust the employment figures for changes in man-hours outside the manufacturing sector. The results for each sector (including the manufacturing sector, already shown in Table 2) are summarized in the following set of regression equations:

Annual rates of growth of productivity (P) and of employment (E) on the rates of growth of output (X)[6]

Industry

    (1) *Manufacturing*

$$P = 1.035 + 0.484X, R^2 = 0.826,$$
$$(0.070)$$
$$E = -1.028 + 0.516X, R^2 = 0.844.$$
$$(0.070)$$

---

[5]It was not possible to separate, on the employment statistics, the distributive trades from banking, insurance, etc. in more than a few cases; but the distributive trades account for much the greater part (around four-fifths or more) of the total output of this sector, and a similar proportion of employment.

[6]Since exponential growth rates have been used throughout, $P + E = X$, and hence the sum of the constants of the two equations should be zero, and the sum of the regression coefficients unity, irrespective of the nature of the correlations involved. However, since estimates of employment growth and of productivity growth have been separately rounded, the sum of these can vary from the total by one decimal point, which explains small deviations from the correct result in some of the pairs of regression equations.

Appendix

(2) *Public utilities* (11 countries, 1953–63)[7]

$$P = 2.707 + 0.419X, R^2 = 0.451,$$
$$(0.154)$$
$$E = -2.690 + 0.577X, R^2 = 0.609.$$
$$(0.154)$$

(3) *Construction* (11 countries, 1953–63)[7]

$$P = -0.543 + 0.572X, R^2 = 0.810,$$
$$(0.092)$$
$$E = 0.552 + 0.428X, R^2 = 0.702.$$
$$(0.092)$$

(4) *Industrial sector as a whole* (12 countries 1953-54–1963–64)

$$P = .888 + 0.446X, R^2 = 0.847,$$
$$(0.060)$$
$$E = -.888 + 0.554, R^2 = 0.893.$$
$$(0.060)$$

Primary sector

(5) *Agriculture* (12 countries, 1953–63)[7]

$$P = 2.700 + 1.041X, R^2 = 0.812,$$
$$(0.155)$$
$$E = -2.684 - 0.056X, R^2 = 0.013.$$
$$(0.155)$$

---

[7]For *public utilities* and *construction,* the equations relate to all countries listed in Table 2, except the Netherlands; the data relate to 1953–63, except for Austria (1951–61), Italy and France (1954–63), Denmark and Canada (1955–63). The same holds for *agriculture,* except that here the Netherlands (1953–63) is also included. The estimates on *mining* exclude Austria and Denmark; they relate to 1955–64, except for Netherlands where they relate to 1955–61.

Appendix

(6) *Mining* (10 countries, 1955–64)[7]

$$P = 4.0714 + 0.671X, \ R^2 = 0.705,$$
$$(0.153)$$
$$E = -4.0714 + 0.329X, \ R^2 = 0.365.$$
$$(0.153)$$

Tertiary sector

(7) *Transport and communications* (9 countries, 1955–64)[8]

$$P = 2.314 + 0.224X, \ R^2 = 0.102,$$
$$(0.252)$$
$$E = -2.314 + 0.776X, \ R^2 = 0.576.$$
$$(0.252)$$

(8) *Commerce* (9 countries, 1955–64)[9]

$$P = -1.751 + 0.953X, \ R^2 = 0.932,$$
$$(0.098)$$
$$E = 1.744 + 0.056X, \ R^2 = 0.044.$$
$$(0.098)$$

The regressions reveal an interesting pattern. In the case of construction and public utilities, the equations relating to both productivity and employment are similar to those in manufacturing, except that in the case of public utilities

---

[8]In the case of *transport and communications,* the estimate excludes Austria, Denmark and Japan; the data relate to 1955–64, except for the U.S.A. (1955–63), France (1956–64) and West Germany (1957–64).

[9]*Commerce* includes G.D.P. originating in wholesale and retail trade, banking, insurance, real estate, at constant prices, and employment relating to the same category, except for Japan where the data on output and employment relate to wholesale and retail trade only. The estimate excludes Austria, Denmark and the Netherlands; it relates to 1955–64, except for Canada (1955–61), U.S.A. (1955–63), West Germany (1957–64) and France (1958–64).

the constant term of the equations is much larger, and hence the significance of the relationship is less, than in the case of either manufacturing or construction.[10] One can thus conclude that the effects of economies of scale on the growth of productivity are significant not only for manufacturing industry but for the industrial sector generally.

Agriculture and mining reveal a different picture. In each case, productivity growth shows a large trend factor which is independent of the growth in total output; the regression coefficient of productivity is not significantly different from unity (except possibly for mining) while the regression for employment is not significantly different from zero for agriculture, and barely significant for mining. In both of these cases productivity growth has exceeded the growth of production for every single country; and the growth in productivity has owed nothing to increasing returns to scale.[11]

---

[10]However in the case of the construction sector there is a *negative* constant term of 0.5 percent a year in the productivity equation, in contrast to manufacturing which shows a positive constant term of 1 percent a year. The reasons for this are likely to be similar to those given below in the discussion of the equations for commerce.

[11]In the case of agriculture the growth of output, for most of the countries considered, has probably been more a reflection of the effects of technological progress and capital investment in raising *yields per acre,* than of the rate of growth of consumer demand. The fact that employment was diminishing in all countries—at a fairly uniform rate of around 2–3½ percent a year—may have simply been the result of the absorption of disguised unemployment, or the reflection of the fact that technological progress has, on the whole, been more labor-saving than land-saving.

Appendix

In the case of transport and communications, there is no correlation whatever between productivity growth and output growth; productivity increased at an independent rate of some 2.3 percent a year (for the average of the nine countries considered) but beyond this any higher rate of growth of output required a corresponding increase in employment (as shown by the regression coefficient of employment on output which is not significantly different from unity). In this case, therefore, productivity growth appears to have been fully autonomous, and owed nothing to economies of scale.

Finally, in the case of commerce, there is a high correlation between productivity growth and output growth (with a regression coefficient not significantly different from unity) but no relation whatever between the growth of employment and of production. The regressions for commerce are remarkably similar to those of agriculture, except for one very important difference: in the case of agriculture there is a large positive constant, showing a trend-rate of increasing productivity, whereas in the case of commerce the trend-rate of growth of productivity is *negative*. This negative trend-rate has nothing to do with technological factors (which operate in the same sort of way in the distributive trades and banking as elsewhere—as, for example, the development of supermarkets or mechanization) but is mainly a reflection of the peculiar manner in which competition operates in this field, tending constantly to eliminate abnormal profits through a multiplication of units, rather than through a reduction of prices or distributive margins. These estimates confirm the view that while an increase in the total turnover of banking or the distributive trades automatically raises productivity

Appendix

(i.e. turnover per employee) the inflow of labor into these trades is not directly connected with the rise in turnover.

(c) The Role of Investment in Productivity Growth

It was suggested in the text that deviations from the "Verdoorn Law" in the industrial sector were correlated with investment behavior. This hypothesis has been tested by means of multiple regressions which include the gross investment/output ratio, (expressed as a percentage) as a measure of investment behavior.

Because data on gross asset formation in the manufacturing sector were not obtainable for all countries, these estimates refer to the industrial sector, which is defined as manufacturing plus construction plus public utilities. For this sector the "Verdoorn equations" as shown in equation (4) above are:

Industrial Sector (12 countries, 1953-54–1963-64)

(1) $\quad P = .888 + .446X, R^2 = .847,$
$\qquad\qquad (.060)$

(2) $\quad E = -.888 + .554X, R^2 = .893.$
$\qquad\qquad (.060)$

where X, E, and P are the rates of growth of output, employment, and productivity, respectively.

If the gross investment/output ratio is included as a second variable in the equation the following result is obtained:

Industrial Sector (12 countries, 1953-54–1963-64)

(3) $\quad P = .527 + .356X + .048I, R^2 = .880.$
$\qquad\qquad (.079) \quad (.029)$

where I is the gross investment/output ratio in industry, expressed as a percentage.

Appendix

In this equation, the coefficient of I is not statistically significant. However, as stated in the text, Canada, in the period considered, showed abnormal behavior in that she invested very heavily and yet had a very high negative residual calculated from the Verdoorn line. If Canada is excluded from the regression, the following is obtained:

Industrial Sector (11 countries, 1953-54–1963-64)

$$(4) \quad P = .709 + .268X + .073I, R^2 = .960.$$
$$\quad\quad\quad (.047) \quad (.017)$$

which shows that the investment/output ratio has been a significant factor in determining the rate of growth of productivity, for these countries.

The influence of the rate of growth of employment and of the investment/output ratio has been further investigated using a somewhat different approach,—i.e. by regarding the rate of growth of output as the dependent variable, and the rate of growth of employment and the investment/output ratio as the independent variables. The implication of the Verdoorn Law in this case is that the regression coefficient on the rate of growth of employment is significantly greater than unity. As is shown below, this remains true even if a multiple regression is used, allowing for the influence of investment as well as employment, on output.

For the twelve countries, a simple regression gives the following result (which is of course implied by the Verdoorn equations above):

Industrial Sector (12 countries 1953-54–1963-64)

$$(5) \quad X = 2.06 + 1.614E, R^2 = .893.$$
$$\quad\quad\quad (.176)$$

Appendix

In a simple regression the value of R^2 is unaffected by an interchange of the independent and dependent variables, and for high values of R^2 the estimates of the regression coefficients are not significantly altered (the coefficient of X on E obtained algebraically from regression (2) above comes to 1.80.)

A multiple regression of the rate of growth of output on the rate of growth of employment and the gross investment/output ratio gives the following equation for the full sample of twelve countries:

Industrial Sector (12 countries, 1953-54–1963-64)

(6) $X = .835 + 1.367E + .097I$, $R^2 = .940$.
               (.168)   (.037)

and if Canada is excluded:

(7) $X = .937 + 1.320E + .105I$, $R^2 = .986$.
               (.085)   (.018)

Both these regressions show that there is a significant partial correlation between the rate of growth of output and the gross investment/output ratio. It should be noted that the inclusion of the investment/output ratio, while it decreases the coefficient on the rate of growth of employment, does not alter the conclusion that this coefficient is significantly greater than unity; which implies that the rate of growth of productivity is positively correlated with the rate of growth of output and also with the rate of growth of employment.